MORBID
CURIOSITIES

MORBID CURIOSITIES

·

Derek Pell

JONATHAN CAPE
THIRTY BEDFORD SQUARE LONDON

Some of these works first appeared in the following publications: *Beatniks from Space, Benzene, Bizarre Angel, Black Veins, Bogg, Caprice, Fly by Night, Helix, Montana Gothic, Not Guilty, Only Paper Today, Peeping Tom, Playboy, Screw* and *Zone*.

'A Man and a Maid with Flowers' and 'Carnal Dreams Revealed' are copyright © 1983 by *Playboy* Magazine.

'How to Write the Suicide Note' and 'How to Slit Your Wrists' are from *Doktor Bey's Suicide Guidebook* (New York, 1977), reprinted by permission of Dodd, Mead & Company, Inc.

'Dok Bey's Physical Fitness Plan for the Dead', 'Dead Body Language' and 'How to Cast Head Forms' are from *Doktor Bey's Book of the Dead* (New York, 1981), reprinted by permission of Avon Books.

'How to Name a Brat' and 'The Strange and Curious Case of Sister Carlotta' are from *Doktor Bey's Book of Brats* (New York, 1979), reprinted by permission of Avon Books.

Text for 'Gertrude Stein's Exercise Plan' is taken from 'Many Many Women', published in *Matisse, Picasso and Gertrude Stein*, Plain Edition, Paris, 1932.

This collection first published 1983
This collection copyright © 1983 by Derek Pell
Previously published pieces copyright © 1977, 1978, 1979, 1980,
1981, 1982, 1983 by Derek Pell
Jonathan Cape Ltd, 30 Bedford Square, London WC1

British Library Cataloguing in Publication Data

Pell, Derek
Morbid curiosities.
I. Title
818'.5409   PS3566.E/

ISBN 0-224-02962-2

Printed in Great Britain by St Edmundsbury Press, Bury St Edmunds, Suffolk

For Marina

CONTENTS

PART I

ETIQUETTE, SELF-HELP AND HOW-TO

FIRST STEP IN MAKING AN ILLUSTRATION FOR THIS BOOK

This is the opium poppy, from which opium is obtained.

This is the artist smoking the opium obtained from the poppy. He will soon be inspired to produce an illustration.

How to do the Socratic Hustle:

Ritual Dance Commemorating the Death of Grecian Disco

Music: Aristophanes and the Birds   Performer: Anonymous Hermaphrodite

Woe together now,
Hustle to the left

Hustle to the right

Shuck right

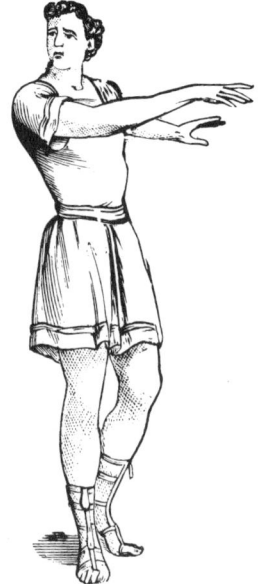

Shuck left,
Swindle on down

Rip up,
Rip down,
Ripoff together

Bogus to the left

Bogus to the right

Swindle shuck,
Jive sham,
Bogus on down

11

A Guide to Literary Physiognomy of the Sixteenth Century

Hair of a rustic and thick-witted editor and beard of a brutal and overbearing drama critic

Noses of a weak and incompetent publicity director and a vainglorious art director

Mouths of greedy, reckless, lewd and untruthful publishers

Teeth of an over-praised first novelist and an over-looked satirist

Foreheads of irascible, cruel and conniving literary agents

Eyes of an effete essayist and a simple-minded poet

GERTRUDE STEIN'S
EXERCISE PLAN

1 She was placing what she was placing.

2 A little one who could not push did push and pushing was telling that pushing was not succeeding. A little one pushing is a little one pushing.

3 She did tell and she could tell that having had what she had had she would have what she would have, and she did have what she did have and she did tell what she did tell.

4 In continuing she did not change when she was remaining in having been moving being sitting. She was not sitting in the way of sitting.

5   They were losing in coming and they were coming to be
    intending.

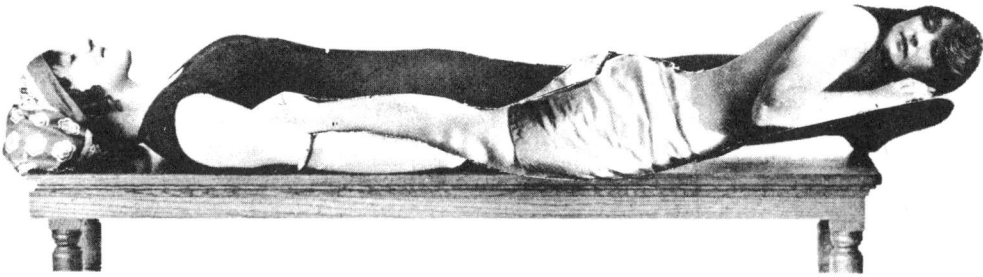

6   She was needing being one living to be feeling what she was
    feeling in having the one, in having the other one.

7   She repeated that in liking what she had been liking she had, in
    giving what she had been giving, been having what she had.

8   She was doing more than she intended and she liked it.

THE BRAVE BATTLE FOR WOMEN'S RIGHTS

Salute Position 1

Salute Position 2

Salute Position 3

Salute Position 4

The Grand Salute

On Guard

Reading for a Beautiful Bosom

Reading can be the key to a beautiful bosom, regardless of your size. Whether you are small, full-figured, or somewhere in between, a good programme of reading can achieve several benefits for you. The first is to improve your posture. Reading while standing erect, a hardback held at arm's length from the chest, with shoulders relaxed, will help delineate a petite pair, raise a sagging bustline, and separate abundant orbs to minimize their size. The heavier the volume employed, the greater the benefits of chest-stretch. An oversized Bible held with both hands at head level can firm up the bosom miraculously! Lightweight mass-market paperbacks, one in each hand, may be read (skimmed) alternately while turning the head from one to the other and lowering the arms upon completion of each page. Moreover, speedreading a sentence from the left book to the right one, back and forth, until both pages of each volume have been digested, albeit combined, can tone up those pectoral muscles which support your breasts to give your bosom a higher, firmer, more intelligent appearance.

Another benefit of a carefully prepared programme of reading: better proportions generally. Are your bosom and hip measurements nearly the same, your waist ten inches smaller? If not, try using a hardback and paperback simultaneously; juggle them over your head for ten minutes, then pause and read a paragraph from either one. Switch books without losing your place. Now try to remember what you have read while placing the volumes under your arms and squeezing with your elbows. Presto! You will have brought these measurements into correct proportion.

So come on girls, start reading!

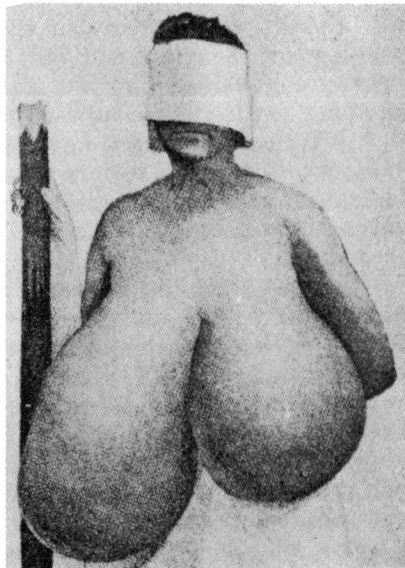

A CELIBATE'S LEXICON: A HANDY GUIDE

ADULTERY Celibacy, as practised by children.

BED Piece of furniture for the purpose of *sexual intercourse* (see *perversion*). Most celibates prefer a bed of nails.

BYESEXUAL Man who has bid farewell to his private parts (see *castration*).

CASTRATION Removal, by chisel, of unwanted protuberance.

CHASTITY BELLS Device that, when attached to the genitalia of either sex, warns of the slightest arousal in time to take preventative action (see *shower bathing*).

CLAP Sound of celibate expressing joy.

DATA Gossip exchanged by celibates.

DISEASE That which is not contracted by celibates, with the exception of leprosy.

EJACULATE One who flees the altar prior to saying 'I will.'

FRIDGE Female celibate; miniature igloo enclosing the clitoris.

GAY CELIBATE One who travels exclusively in mixed company.

IMPOTENCE Motto among Southern celibates: 'Sex is of no impotence.'

JAPANESE STYLE Suicide performed on one's wedding night.

KNOWLEDGE (CARNAL) That which is unknown.

LIMA BEANS Celibate's favourite snack.

LUBRICATION Greasing one's feet (or footwear) to aid in escape from a rapist.

MASOCHIST A well-adjusted celibate.

MISSIONARY POSITION Standing erect in the middle of a jungle.

NAVEL Object of contemplation among devout celibates.

ORAL CONTRACEPTIVE A lecture on the joy of celibacy.

ORGAN DONOR See *castration*.

PERVERSION See *sexual intercourse*.

PIMP Dwarf devoted to the seduction of celibates.

21

QUICKIE Competition among celibates in the fifty-metre dash.

RAILWAYS Transportation avoided by male celibates for fear of entering a tunnel.

SADIST An unhappy celibate.

SALTPETER Aphrodisiac for virgins.

SELF-ABUSE The banging of one's head against a wall to vent hostility.

SEXUAL INTERCOURSE See *perversion*.

SHOWER BATHING Simultaneous cold shower and hot bath to exorcise desire.

SIXTY-NINE Number of non-erogenous zones.

TESTICLE Phallic-shaped frozen dessert given those entering a convent to establish their sincerity.

UNDERWEAR See *chastity bells*.

VASECTOMY The placement of an urn over the male member to conceal an erection.

VOYEUR A blind celibate.

WET BLANKET Lounging robe for celibates ('Excuse me, while I slip into something less comfortable').

Castration

The Auto-Abuser

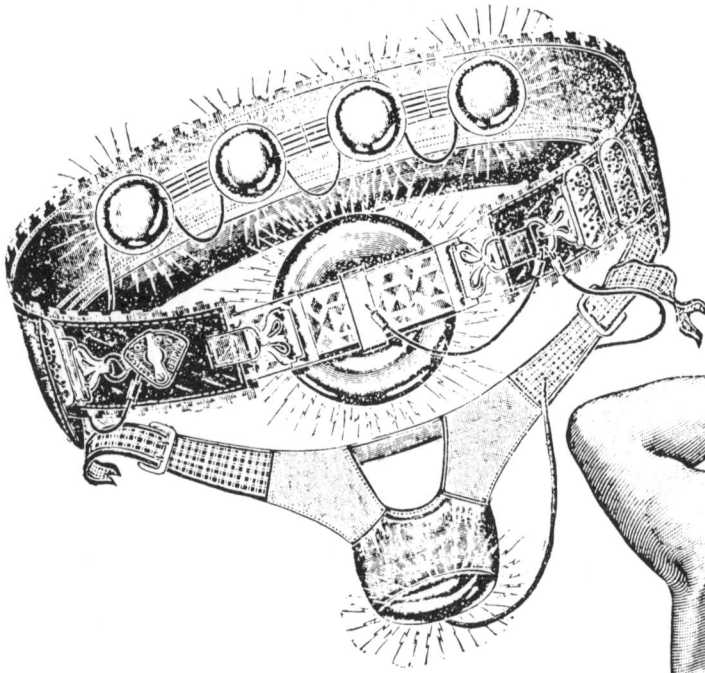

'Look, Mum, no hands'

Whether worn under one's clothes for an outing at the track or in the privacy of the study, the Auto-Abuser permits carefree, hygienic bliss.

A most ingenious creation, it comes complete with an electra-belt and crotch harness, enabling one to climax indoors or out.

How to Write the Suicide Note

1   Use of the first person is generally preferred.

2   For maximum impact and credibility, always write in the past tense. (Example: I *was* a failure in business.)

3   If you are without family, friends, or even enemies, address the note 'To Whom It May Concern.'

4   When possible, use a typewriter. Far too many notes are indecipherable.

5   Keep a carbon copy in your pocket, in case the original is misplaced.

6   Do not concern yourself with the 'beginning-middle-end' rule. Just concentrate on the end.

7   Remember that these are your last words. They should be commensurate with your social position. They should reverberate in the reader's mind! Avoid such clichés as 'Goodbye cruel world' and 'To be or not to be . . .' Strive for the poetic.

8   Self-pity, slang and obscenity are acceptable.

9   If artistically inclined, attach a self-portrait.

10   Be brief. Nothing is more boring than a long goodbye.

How to Slit Your Wrists

1   Use a freshly sharpened butcher's knife or small axe, though when employing the latter, be careful to stroke *lightly*.

2   Draw a line on the wrist(s) just below the cuff-wrinkle (see diagram).

3   Hold your implement in whichever hand is most comfortable (if you cannot decide, use the eeny-meeny-miny-mo selection process) and position the sharp edge of the blade four inches above the line you have drawn.

4   Take a deep breath.

5   Now, as gracefully as possible, slice with the blade across the line, penetrating the flesh by at least a quarter of an inch. The stroke should be even. *Do not use a sawing or hacking motion.*

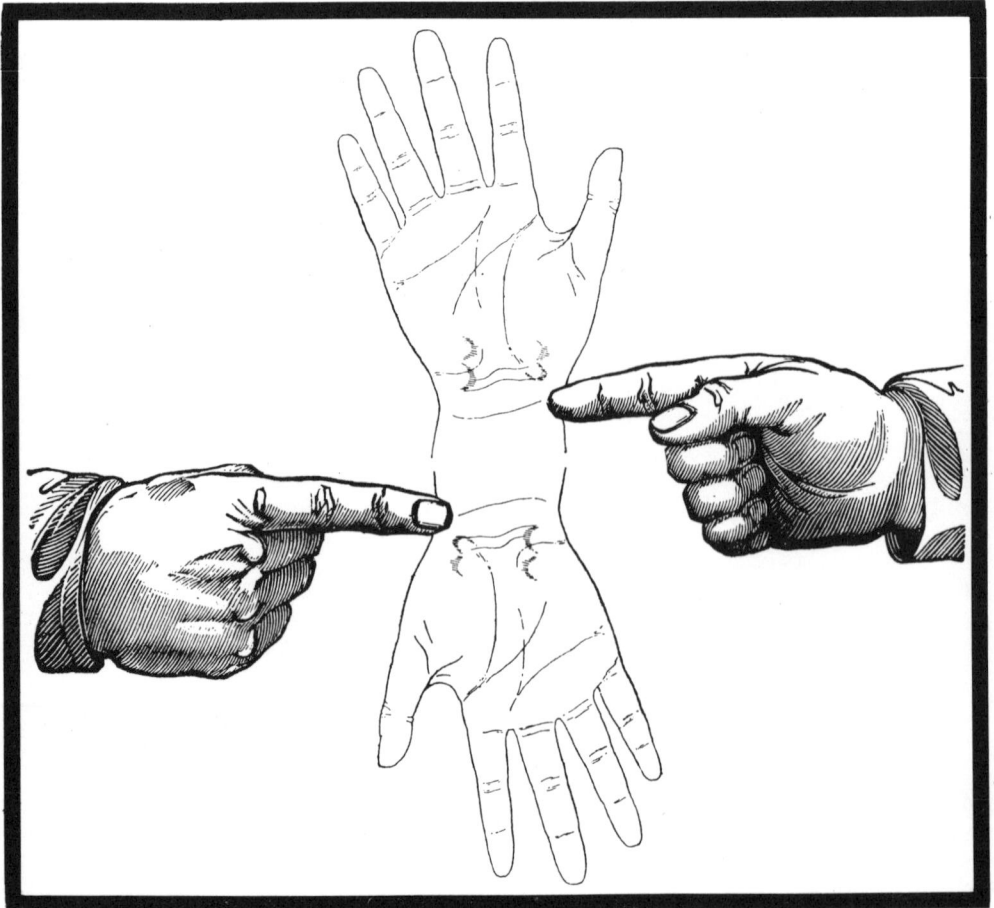

6   Bleed.

Dok Bey's Physical Fitness Plan for the Dead

It was during a short-lived stay in Canada that I made a surprising discovery — the entire population of Quebec had passed away. It was a fact I could easily have lived with, had it not been for the contemptible condition of the deceased citizens. Without exception, they had allowed their remains to lie idly by in a sordid celebration of sloth! Everywhere I went I saw *flabby* cadavers just killing time (presumably waiting for dodot),* bloated beyond diet. Not even among the population of New Jersey does one find such a total *lack of self-respect.*

Upon my return to our civilized isle, I developed the following six-point programme** of fitness for stiffs. If practised daily, for ever, these simple exercises are guaranteed to keep a dead body in tiptop shape from head to toe.

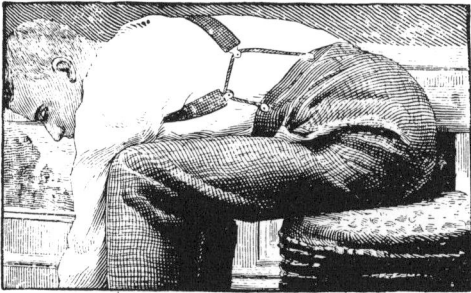

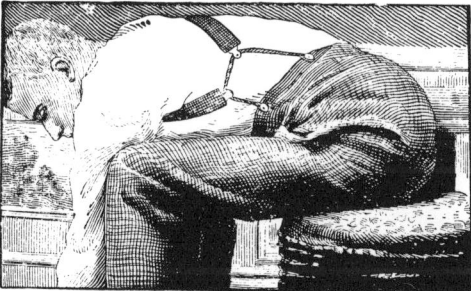

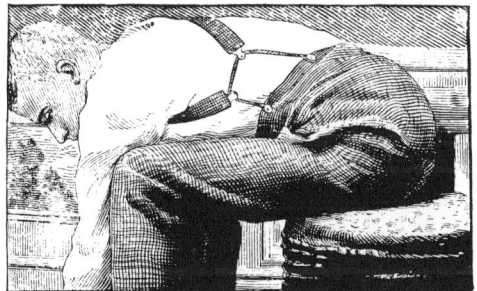

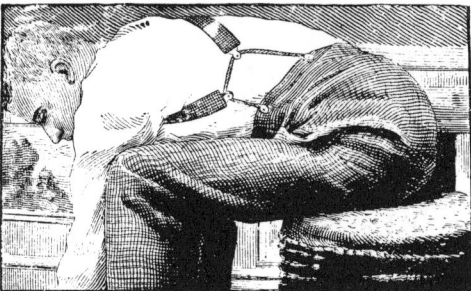

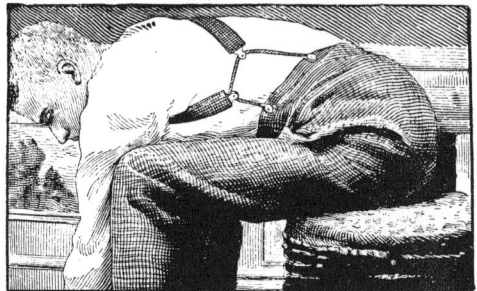

*A mythological bird of prey.

**I had originally called my plan *The Royal Canadian No-Air Exercises.* This name, while poetic, seemed too provincial to pay off and, thus, has been omitted.

Dead Body Language

(female)

A shroud of silence has, for too long, concealed the hidden personality traits of cadavers. Now, thanks to *necrophysiqueology* (the simple, unscientific study of unconscious physical characteristics), a stiff's true nature is miraculously revealed! The following charts illustrate the most common examples of 'dead body language' and may be used as a handy reference guide at the funeral parlour or stiff-singles' bar.

Fig. 1 Modest; maternal; timid; *fainéante*

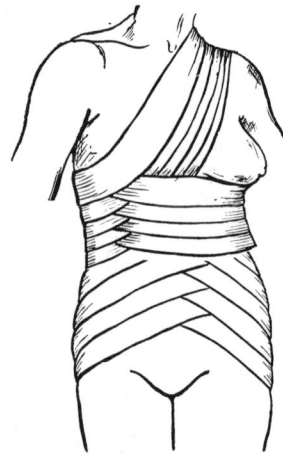

Fig. 2 Immodest; listless; latent; lax

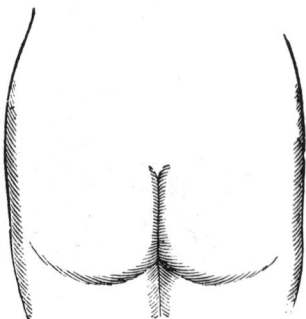

Fig. 3 Modest; cheerful; feckless; fey

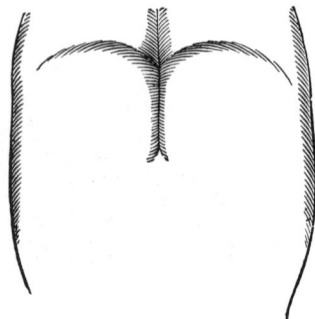

Fig. 4 Immodest; gloomy; fickle; inverted

Dead Body Language

(male)

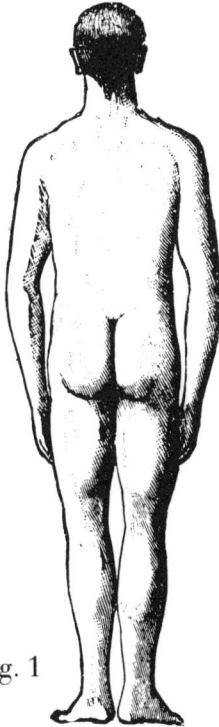

Fig. 1

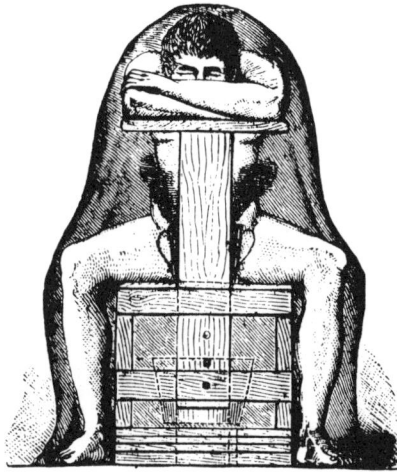

Fig. 3

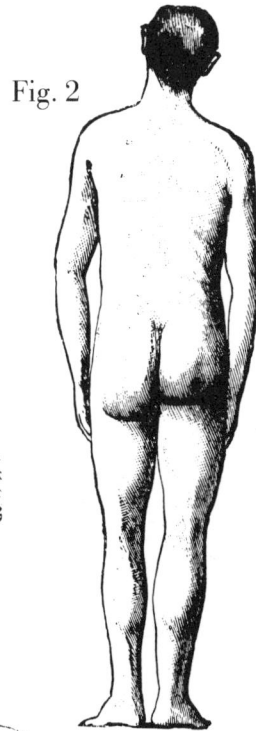

Fig. 2

Fig. 4

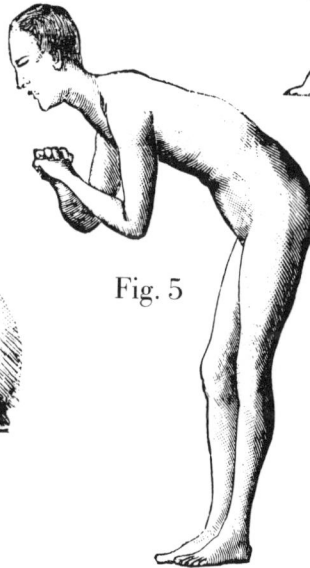

Fig. 5

Fig. 1 Prepared for all eventualities; cocksure; quiet; naive
Fig. 2 Prone to inferiority; indolent; cynical; chip on shoulder
Fig. 3 'The Dreamer': slothful; sheepish; untrustworthy
Fig. 4 'The Thinker': shallow; shiftless; lymphatic; tardy
Fig. 5 Pious; upright; sluggish; hypocritical*

*Ex-member of the Immortal Majority

How to Shake Hands with the Common Man

1   Approach CM with head held high and look directly into his eyes to establish your trustworthiness. Avoid all expressions of contempt or condescension. Remember, for the moment you are equals.

2   Place left hand on CM's shoulder and say, 'Hello there, sir, my name is ——— and I'm running for ———. I trust I can depend on your support.'

3   Before startled CM can reply, grab hold of his left hand and squeeze firmly.

4   Shake the hand up and down three times while admiring the CM's wrist.

5   Open palm and slide your hand between his thumb and forefinger. Wiggle fingers.

6   Grasp CM's thumb firmly in your fist; rotate hand and grip his palm near wrist. Thrust arm forward and report: 'I'm the underdog in this campaign.'

7   Step back one pace with left foot, open palm and raise left elbow overhead. Say, 'It's an uphill battle, but with *your* help I think we can defeat the corrupt Mr ———.'

8   Thrust left arm forward under CM's chin and nudge gently. Smile with sincerity.

9   Always beware of opposition party zealots.

1

2

3

4

5

6

7

8

9

HOW TO CAST HEAD FORMS

FOR PURPOSE OF MOUNTING, HEAD FORMS ARE SOMETIMES EXTREMELY VALUABLE

HEAD IS IMBEDDED ONE HALF IN A BOX OF FINE WET SAND WITH A TIN DAM AROUND ~ A PLASTER MIX IS MADE AND CAREFULLY POURED OVER THE HEAD

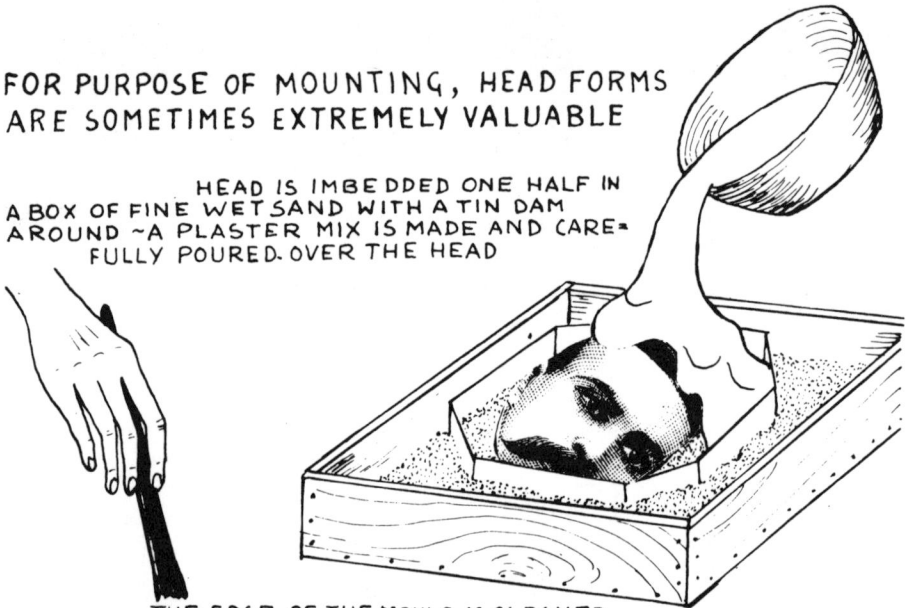

THE EDGE OF THE MOULD IS CLEANED FROM SAND AND THEN BRUSHED WITH SOAP PASTE

SOAP

PLASTER MIX IS POURED OVER THE OTHER SIDE

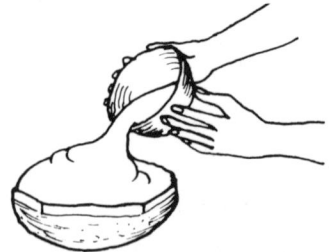

INTERLOCKING KEYS ARE CUT HERE

WHEN ALL IS SET HARD, THE TWO HALVES ARE SPLIT OPEN AND THE HEAD REMOVED

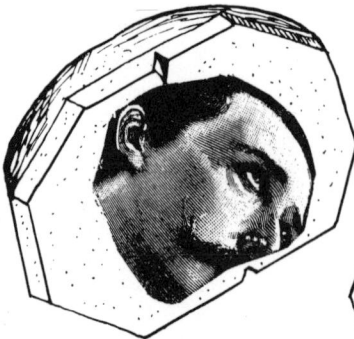

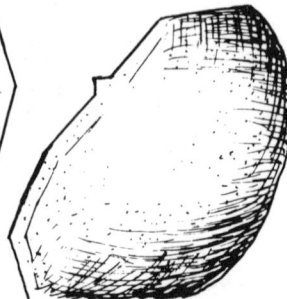

TOSS HEAD ASIDE

32

INTERLUDE I

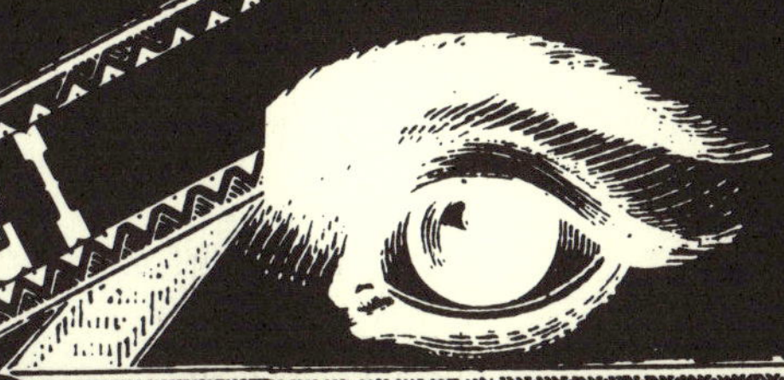

PRETTY PICTURES

The Passionate Toothache

My Country Right or Wrong

Foetal Voyage

FORGOTTEN INVENTORS

& THEIR INVENTIONS

PART II

ELMO 'Hot Lips' HEUNKE

(pronounced 'Hunky'), Bavarian jazz buff and volunteer fire-fighter, combined his avocations to invent the 'Heunke Hero-mantic' – a portable extinguisher and alto sax. This handy gizmo helped boost morale during the Alpine Conflagration of 1769. Alas, both Heunke and his invention proved combustible and perished in the blaze.

38

SIR FREDERIK DISKO

It is a little-known fact that Sir Frederik Disko invented the faddishly popular 'musical hat'. Disko was indeed responsible for the first stereo stovepipe, as well as the rock-and-roller's bowler; the platter-cap; the monaural fedora; and the dolby pith-helmet with reversible echo chamber and woollen woofers. His reverberating headgear disappeared from the scene in 1863 at the time of the deadly migraine epidemic.

Professor Ambruise Poddle and his Biped-Cycle

In 1843 Professor Ambruise Poddle was dismissed from Oxford University for espousing several unorthodox opinions during a lecture on 'Modern Transportation'. Perhaps his most shocking assertion was: 'The invention of the wheel has been absurdly overrated!' At the conclusion of his discourse, amid a crescendo of cat-calls from the audience, the professor unveiled his invention known as the biped-cycle. 'This vehicle', he explained, 'has been designed to improve upon the Oriental rickshaw which, I believe, is rather impersonal, whereas my biped-cycle brings together driver and passenger in harmonious union.' He then announced that he was presently at work on a scaled-down version called the 'Tournament Racist', the chassis of which was composed of a fleetfooted East Indian. 'A real beaut,' proclaimed Poddle.

Unfortunately the professor never lived to see his invention mass produced, as he mysteriously disappeared several weeks later during a cross-country hopscotch competition.

40

Frieda Fryena

The portly daughter of a New Jersey zoo-keeper, Frieda Fryena dedicated her life to inventing appliances for pets. At the age of eighteen, when most girls are busy necking in parked cars, Frieda was circulating a petition demanding 'more leisure time for animals' – part of her campaign for Pets' Rights. Armed with over seven signatures and a rucksack stuffed with sandwiches, she marched from her home in Lodi to the State House in Trenton, where she was arrested for chaining a chimpanzee to the Governor. This setback, however, did not deter Frieda Fryena. In 1932, she opened an exclusive mail-order operation, Frieda's House of Fur, which offered a wide range of unusual gifts, including a mint-flavoured mouthwash for parakeets; a hammock for horses; a battery-operated dog bone burier; a whirlpool bath for tropical fish; and a de luxe combination cat litter and miniature golf course. Unfortunately, the House of Fur did not survive the Great Depression and Frieda Fryena went off to war.

Automatic Q-Tip for Elephants

BUSTER KÄRP

Buster Karp, a jeweller from Dubuque,* was best known as the father of fish trinkets and the creator of such oddities as quasi-precious trout bangles, mackerel anklets, tuna tiepins, oyster chains, herrings, bass rings, barracuda cameos, octopi wedding rings and the blowfish brooch. Often oversized, Karp's gems were lovely to look at but utterly impractical.

*Karp, coincidentally, lived next door to Boris Cornsmog (see page 47).

GERUNAMUCK

An underrated member of the famed Apache Indians, Gerunamuck (alias 'The Unlucky One') began his career as an inventor in 1882 with the construction of Big Skyscrapper, a twelve-storey teepee. He went on to develop the first powwowminium and the totem pole booth; the latter being a carved enclosure in which one could transmit long-distance smoke-signals. His most popular creation was the covered doghouse (shown above), which was easily transported during attacks by the White Man. Gerunamuck's final invention was, alas, a fatal one: a curved tomahawk he called the doomerang.

JACQUES ROTSEAU

French founder of the Odourrealist Movement. Jacques Rotseau held his first public exhibition in Paris in 1894. His fetid murals and scratch-and-sniff sculptures were dismissed by critics and 'connoisewers' alike. Rotseau's controversial canvas, 'Skunk Descending a Staircase', was removed from the gallery and burned in the street by rival Aromaticists. This ill-fated début led the artist to patent Master-Ban, a roll-on deodorant for use with his works.

Odourrealists at work

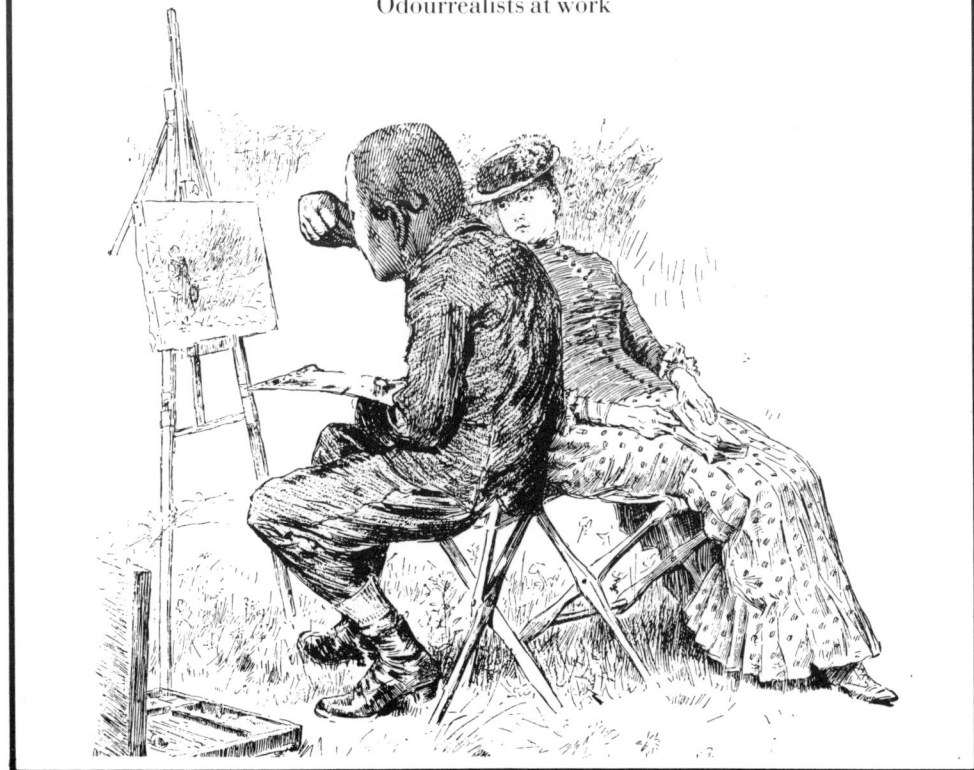

Professor Hurley's Sewage Scooter

After countless test 'runs', Professor Burl Hurley presented his mobile toilet to the world. Although crude in concept, the sewage scooter was highly praised for its economical design, as it converted the driver's waste matter into gas and was thus propelled. When human fuel was unavailable, common footpower was employed. Hurley's invention was aimed at 'the man on the go' and was not considered decorous transport for females. Several models were available for purchase, including the inexpensive S.S. 2 go-cart; the De Luxe Bowlmobile (fig. 1, side view); and the speedy Pot Rod (fig. 2, rear view). In addition, Professor Hurley offered a line of accessories not included in the purchase price: roll bar; magazine rack; yellow snow tyres; wipers; air freshener (with pump); and rear-view mirror.

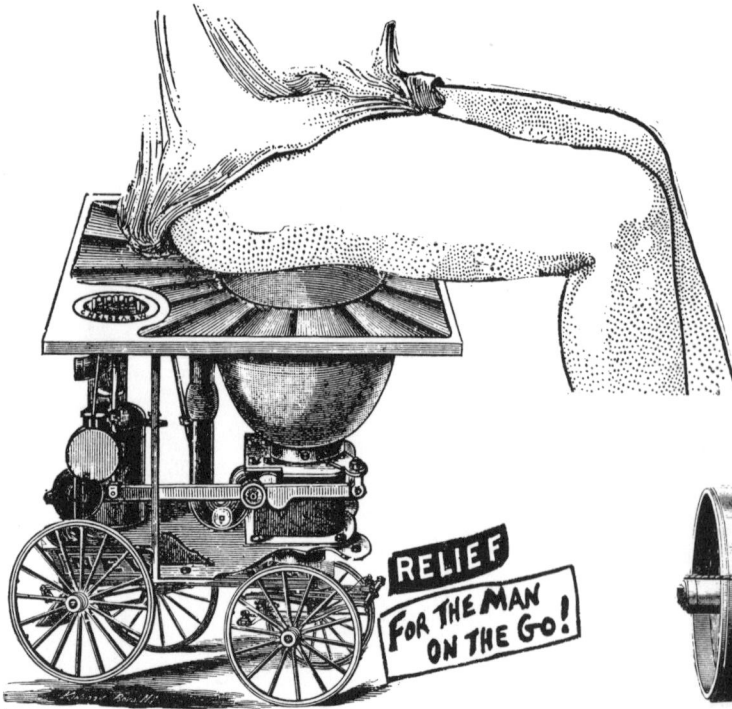

RELIEF FOR THE MAN ON THE GO!

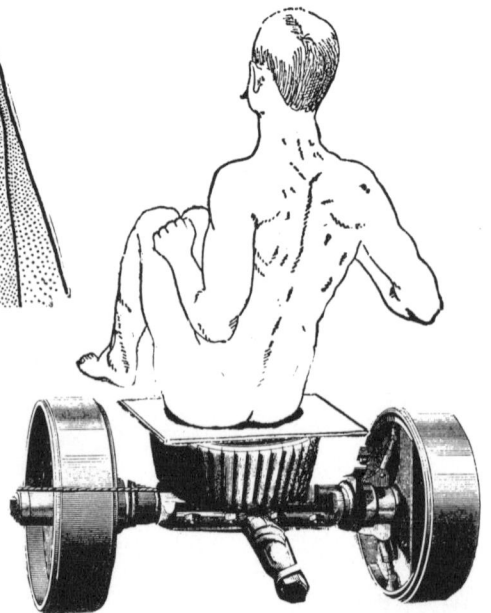

Fig. 1

Fig. 2

BORIS CORNSMOG

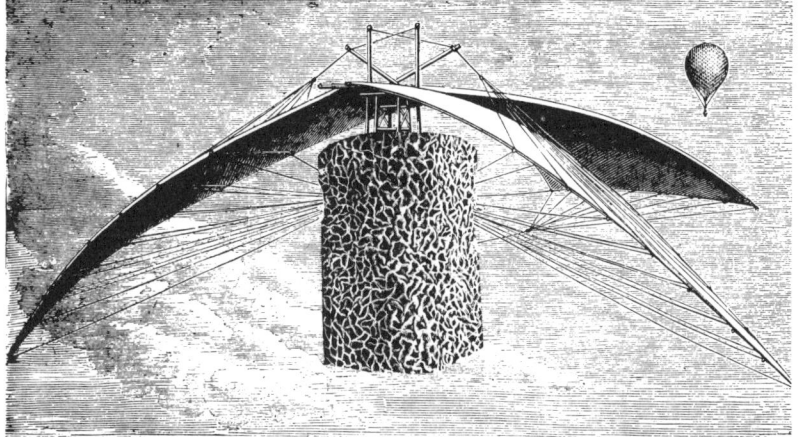

Boris Cornsmog, a deranged meteorologist from Iowa, became obsessed with the desire to put a stop to precipitation. He was frequently overheard remarking to himself, 'Everybody talks about the rain, but nobody ever does anything about it!' In an effort to improve the weather, Cornsmog launched his aerosponge in 1895. In fact, the aircraft was successful in absorbing a large quantity of rainfall; however, the additional weight led to its descent. Subsequent to the crash, Cornsmog lost his life in a mob of irate farmers.

DR JARVIS JIGGLE

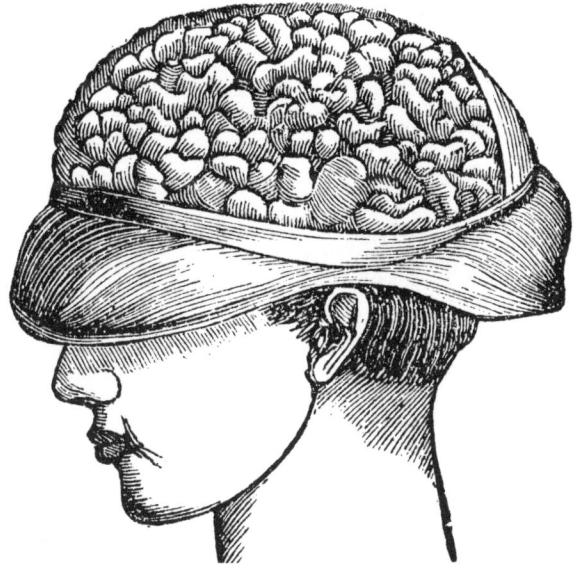

During the performance of a slipshod lobotomy, Dr Jarvis Jiggle inadvertently invented the skullcap (1892).

THE McTWITTLE BROTHERS

Raised by a pair of itinerant sissies, Bo and Lenny McTwittle grew up to champion the cause of pacifism in America. Both men were accomplished escape artists and knew how to vote with their feet. In 1889, Lenny, the larger of the two, attained employment as a long-shoreman in New York. His first day on the job, he attempted to teach his co-workers a sport of his own invention: pacifisticuffs (which came to be called shadow-boxing). This endeavour met with little enthusiasm and, consequently, Lenny was forced to run for his life. Meanwhile, his brother Bo had manufactured the world's first non-violent handgun: the Sunday-morning Special (see below).

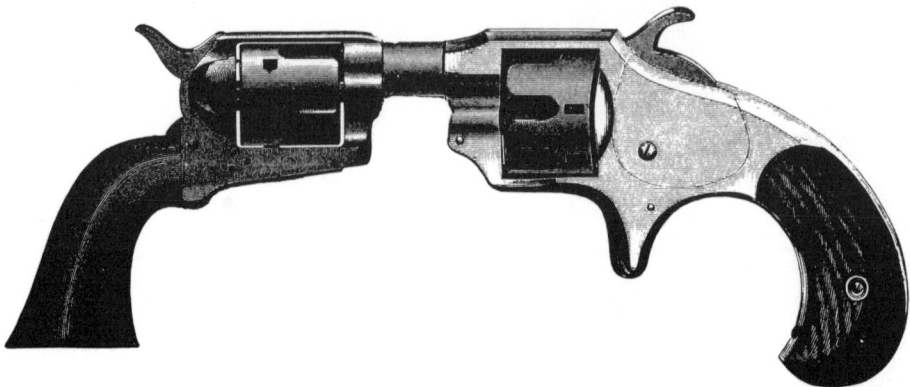

BELA & BUCK FEELEY

Without Bela and Buck Feeley, there might never have been a Masters and Johnson. Much maligned during their lifetimes, the Feeleys fought repressive Victorian morality at their secluded clinic in Cambridge. There they encouraged young men and women to engage openly in flirtation. Buck was responsible for instructing the males in the art of whispering sweet nothings, while Bela taught the females how to expose their ankles in daylight. The Feeleys were most interested in the physiology of blushing and published a number of important texts on the subject. Together they invented a centripetal apparatus to aid students in overcoming their guilt and shyness: the Sweetheart Snuggle Tank. At a public demonstration of the SST, Buck and Bela were arrested for 'wantonly disorienting adolescent morals'.

GASPAR 'That's not funny' NIX

Possessed of an unpleasant visage and severe personality defects, Gaspar Milstone Nix suffered a painful adolescence. Not only was he subjected to cruel pranks at the hands of his classmates, but he was even the object of ridicule at home, where he was required to don a dunce cap at dinner. For seven years he slept in a short-sheeted bed, never once suspecting mischief. On his thirteenth birthday, poor Gaspar spent the whole day trying to extinguish a trick candle implanted in a cupcake. At school, he was so often the victim of 'hotfoot' that he was forced to wear snowshoes in spring. Upon reaching maturity, Gaspar Nix had a chip on his shoulder the size of a water-melon and thus resolved to devote his remaining days to thwarting practical jokers. Never again would he permit a rubber snake or dribble-glass to get the best of him. 'You won't have Gaspar Nix to kick around any more!' he announced to no one in particular. In 1925, he patented his most ingenious invention: a foolproof whoopie-cushion detector (based on experiments by Hans Geiger).

Whoopie-cushion Detector

50

INTERLUDE II

PICTURES

MORE PRETTY

Quentin's Revenge

A Day at the Zoo

A Day at the Circus

The End of Summer

The Début

Sunday Afternoon

Adolescence

PLEASANT DREAMS

PART IIII

Carnal Dreams *Revealed*

by Doktor Bey, Pataphysician

I have always been bewitched by the secrets of sleep and, most particularly, the capacity of the human mind to conjure up fantastic carnal dramas. As a boy I could hardly wait for my bedtime to arrive, for it was then that I went to that private screening-room inside my skull to view Zzz-rated features. However, upon awakening, I was often faced with the frustration of being unable to recall those fleeting erotic images. Thus, a determined desire somehow to preserve my own dreams led me to begin experimentation which has now resulted in the invention of my Video-Dream Synthesizer – a machine which enables one to both *record* and *play back* naughty nocturnal visions. This unique process permits multiple viewings of the unexpurgated dream with *no commercial interruptions*. And although it remains impossible to run the images in reverse, fast/forward operation is presently being perfected (a useful feature for passing rapidly through unwanted nightmares). Permit me to describe briefly my machine's operation.

The V-D Synthesizer is a patacomputer comprised of sixty-nine fantasy-sensors (*sinsors*), a drive-in memory bank, carnal brain-wave measuring apparatus, magic lantern, and pontine cell projection circuits; to this central unit is connected a cranial helmet lined with a crenellated platinum skullcap (*dream beanie*), the teeth of which are clamped into the scalp of a sleeping subject. Metal side-plates wired to a magnetic 'cage' reproduce and transmit the electrical *sinpulses* and oscillations from previously implanted electrodes. In addition, an EEG (Erect Electro-Geiger) suction-duct with galvanized rubber *smut-pump* (containing its own lecher circuit) is plugged directly into the dreamer's cortex, acting as a 'sin tunnel' for the highly charged carnal brain-waves (*craves*) to pass through. The *craves* are subsequently speed-fed into the Synthesizer's self-cranking nocturnal porn-transformer (a.k.a. 'Emissions Control') and appear as pulsating CDs (Consciousness Dots) on a trilateral scan-screen where they are instantly analized for precise density, colour, shape, and soundtrack. Finally, the un-edited raw brain-footage (*crainage*) encased in its horny dream-skin is then *transanimated* into hundreds of separate *napshots* (a.k.a. 'stills') and projected (via magic lantern) on to a clean white sheet.

On the following pages is reproduced a selection of sample *napshots* from the dreams of several dirty-minded donors who permitted me and my assistant* to bug them during their REM (Ribald Eye Movement) periods. I have provided data for each dream, including title, running time and a brief plot summary for the purpose of future rentals.

Pleasant dreams indeed!

*Sir Lloyd Boyd-Froyd, seen wearing cranial helmet (raincoat on lap not shown).

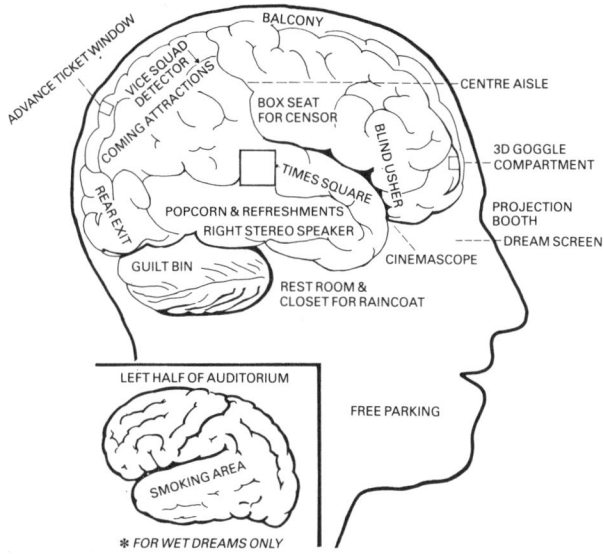

Figure 73 **THEATRE OF THE BRAIN**

Figure 71

Figure 72

Fig. 71 depicts interior of dreamer's skull during performance of *Lady Godiva Goes to Vegas*.

Fig. 72 shows layout of advanced projection booth.

Fig. 382 Lustful subject seen during intense REM phase, screening a sneak-preview of *Ursula the Slut*.

Fig. 422 CBW (carnal brain-wave = *crave*) transformed to heated climax-spiral which is then broken down into (fig. 386) CDs (Consciousness Dots) prior to final invasion of privacy.

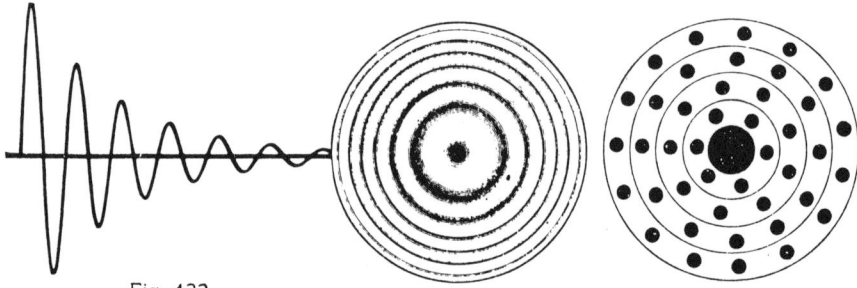

Fig. 422

Fig. 386

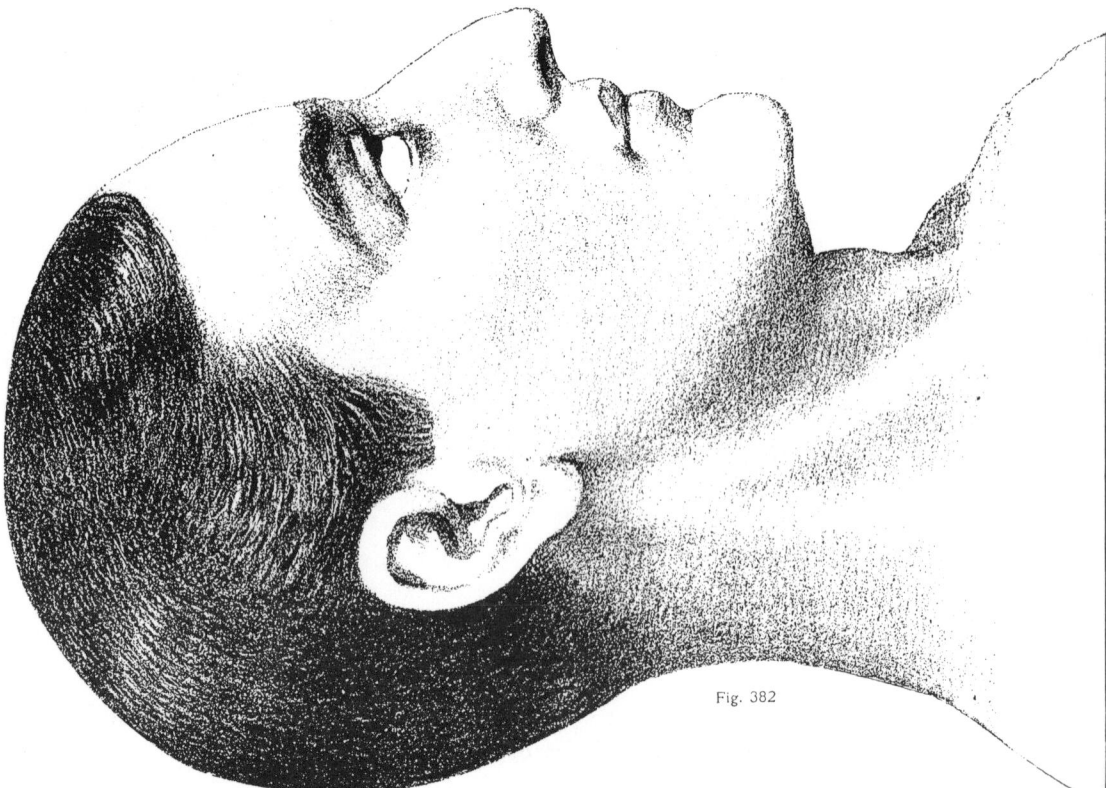

Fig. 382

A carnal dream in progress may be detected by a series of quickie eye exertions in which the sleeper's peepers leap up and down, dart lewdly left and right, and bulge in the throes of *somnambulust*. This phase, known as REM (Ribald Eye Movement), was discovered in 1842 by the Italian dreamophiliac Snorico Snuzzini, who immediately declared the condition 'la creama dreama'.

R.E.M.* CHART
* RIBALD EYE MOVEMENT

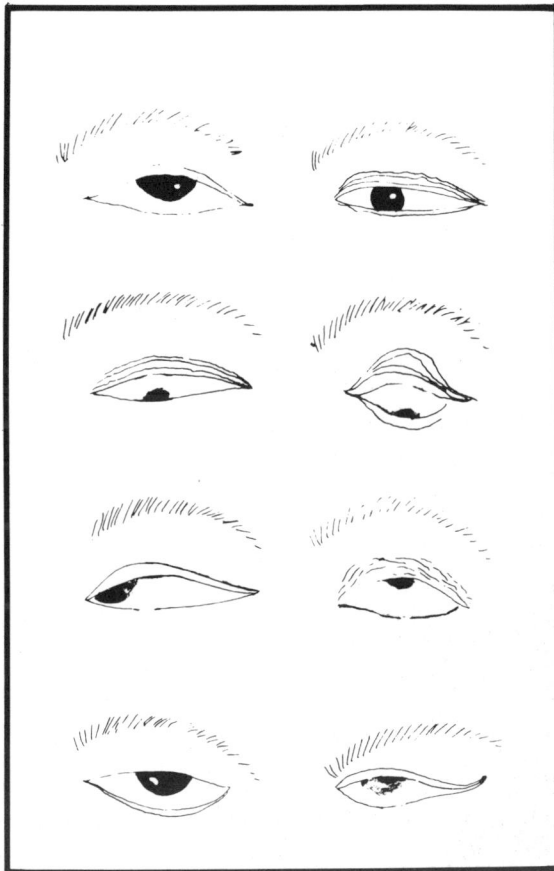

The above chart illustrates common optic activity during REM cycle of the popular dream *Lolita's Younger Sister* (1852).

SELECTED NAPSHOTS

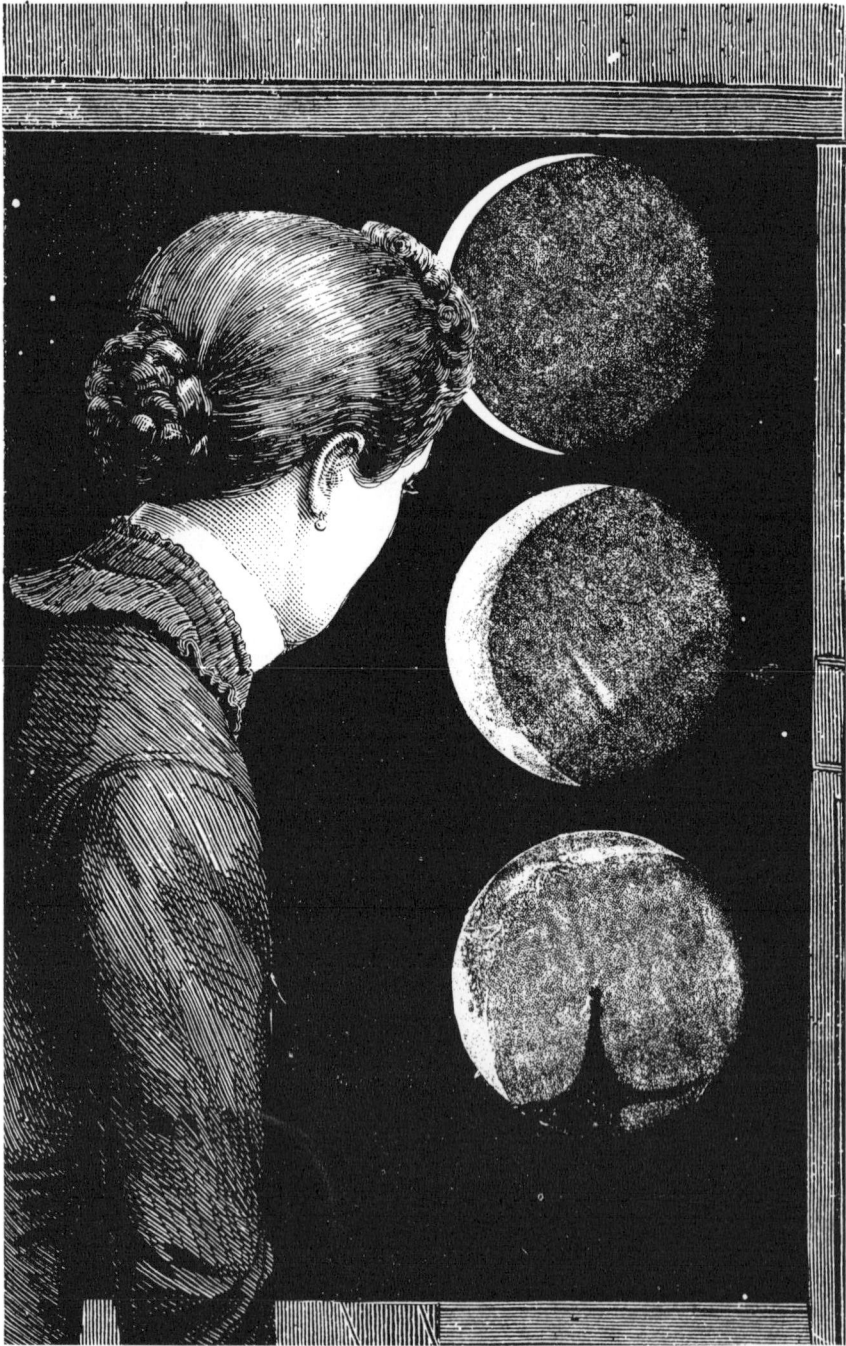

THE MOON IS DOWN   (Running time: 45 sec.)

A fast-paced, somewhat asinine low-budget sleeper. Popular among university students and astronomers.

THREE INTO TWO WON'T GO (Running time: 42 sec.)

Thwarted and confused vision of two loose women and one dizzy hermaphrodite. Attempts at slapstick fail miserably.

THE ICEMAN COMETH   (Running time: 32 min.)

Original title: *Story of O°* A chilling drama common to frigid Eskimos.
Features the longest-running orgasm ever imagined.

SERVICING THE MAID   (Running time: 36 sec.)

This short-subject, originally titled *Upstairs, Backstairs*, is an exciting vision shared by wealthy Englishmen and celibate puppeteers.

STAR WHORES   (Running time: 17 min.)

A high-flying maiden is assaulted by a phalactic spacecraft and later begs for more. Popular dream among disgruntled virgins.

TO HAVE AND TO HOLD   (Running time: 90 min.)

A vibrant love story about a female exhibitionist and her battery-powered paramour.

THE RAPE OF THE LOCK (Running time: 1 min. 43 sec.)

A common dream among militant suffragettes and effeminate Popes. Not to be confused with *The Rape of Lucrece*, a dull softcore documentary.

BANQUET DREAM   (Running time: 9 min.)

Common among repressed gourmets and latent eunuchs, the plot revolves around the protagonist's anxiety over correct table manners ('the etiquette complex').

LITTLE HOSE ON THE PRAIRIE
(Running time: 21 sec.)
A not-so-hot spaghetti western, featuring a short-lived affair between a retired fire superintendent and a disappointed saloon girl. Dubbed.

Dans la tristesse et dans l'amour

MAGIC TWANGER, MON AMOUR

(Running time: 10 min.)

This classic French wet-dream concerns a woman's passion for well-hung amphibians. Subtitles.

HE SPIED HER WITH BOOT ON   (Running time: 90 sec.)

This clumsily titled, fast-paced drama has been frequently screened by both voyeurs and foot-fetishists. Signifies either an advanced case of aesthete's foot fungus or a transatlantic voyage.

INTERLUDE III

PRETTY PICTURES

YET MORE

The Invention of Music

Summer Camp

The Invasion

Mummy Doesn't Live Here Any More

PART IV

Bedtime Stories

Short Story of 0

Here is the final revised first chapter to the infamous novel by Pauline Réage which, until now, has been suppressed. In this laconic, less lascivious version we find René frustrated by his young lover's negative frame of mind.

Her lover one day takes O for a walk in a section of the city where they never go — Montsouris Park. After they have taken a stroll and have sat together side by side on the edge of a lawn, they notice, at the corner of the park, a car which, because of its meter, resembles a taxi.

'Get in,' he says.

'No,' says O.

The Strange and Curious Case
of Sister Carlotta

In 1857, at a nunnery north of Rome, Sister Carlotta Luccia Wyamea awoke one night from a troubled sleep. The Mother Superior arrived at her bedside and became quite concerned upon noticing an odd distension at the top of the young nun's habit.

'And what is this, my child?' inquired the abbess who, patting the bulge, suspected contraband.

'Don't touch it!' retorted Carlotta, pushing the woman's hand away. 'It *hurts.*'

The abbess listened sceptically as the girl explained the nature of her discomfort as a series of 'heavenly headaches' which had, for months, disturbed her slumber. Distressed by such talk, the Mother Superior summoned a physician from the city. He arrived to discover the nun in great agony, rolling about the floor and mumbling incoherently. He commenced a rather lengthy examination (lasting a fortnight) at the conclusion of which he announced a shocking diagnosis:

'I am afraid you're suffering *with brat* in, of all places, the *cranium.*'

The mortified sister sat in silence as the doctor explained, 'It is, for a woman of your position, better by far to *receive* than to *give.* The result of your selflessness has, you see, gone to your head. In fact,' he added, smiling, 'one might say you've a brat in your belfry.'

'*But that's impossible!*' protested the virgin, angrily, 'Why, I haven't even *seen* a member of your sex for nearly *two years!*'

The physician was nonplussed. The abbess was outraged and immediately ordered the nun away with words that have since become legend.*

A month of arduous travel took our heroine to Paris, where she appeared at the doorway of 110 Rue Morgue, the residence of the re-

*'*Get thee from the nunnery!*'

nowned Belgian bratologist Maurice Dildeaux. Noting with horror the young woman's condition, which in the interval had worsened considerably, Dr Dildeaux invited her in and escorted her to his study. There she began to babble and weep until the physician comforted her with an injection. Calmly, she explained her ordeal and, at the conclusion, said: 'You *must* believe me, Doctor . . . Do you?'

Dildeaux sat for a moment without speaking, his hand to his chin in contemplation. Removing a pen from the desk, he began marking down numbers on a small pad and counting on his fingers.

'What', he asked bluntly, 'are your financial circumstances?'

Carlotta assured him of adequate compensation.

'Well then,' winked Dildeaux, 'I'll accept your tale at face value.'

The next several weeks were devoted to an intense investigation of the expectant skull, during which time the specialist consulted hundreds of tomes, pausing only for nourishment, waste disposal and his daily dose of cocaine. Meanwhile, rumours had begun to circulate in the city, and Sister Carlotta had to be confined to the attic where, through the cracks of the boarded-up window, she observed a crowd of morbid curiosity-seekers.

As the day of delivery drew near, Dildeaux was still without a *modus operandi.*

'It's going to be rough sailing,' he told his patient, eyeing her ill-fitting wimple. Yet despite her macabre cranial proportions, he saw that Carlotta had quite a lovely figure (especially for a nun). For days a certain something had been brewing beneath his dispassionate exterior.

Finally, on the eve of the operation, Maurice and Carlotta sought solace in each other's arms:

'But', she whispered, 'I feel so . . . so unclean.'

'Leave on the head-dress,' said the doctor.

Next morning the hundreds who had maintained an unruly vigil outside were still there, passing bottles of wine back and forth. Inside, Dildeaux looked to the heavens for guidance while Carlotta fainted. No answer was forthcoming so, undeterred, the doctor proceeded to improvise.

Fourteen hours elapsed before the physician emerged from the house looking exhausted and pale. He stepped into the crowd and announced the news of his patient's 'immaculate cranial conception' and the subsequent successful bit of skulldiggery.

'I have performed a most *miraculous* surgery,' he told them, 'which, henceforth, will be known as a *lobratomy*!'

The crowd threw vegetables.

Wearing a plain brown sack over her head, Carlotta escaped by way of the back door. With the brat tucked beneath her habit she ran to a nearby orphanage where, for an outlandish fee, the disposal was transacted.

Carlotta Luccia Wyamea never saw her saviour again for he expired at the hands of the mob. Her saga concluded in California where she settled the following year. There she publicly denounced her Catholicism and formed a cult of her own.

Position of Parts

'She is lying on her right side, the upper part of her body half flung back so as to turn her face up into the camera. The right arm is stretched the length of her body while the left arm is raised over head hiding the ear but giving a good view of the downy armpit and the breast. The legs are bent, the right one slightly and the left much more, the knee pulled way up. From the way the picture was taken and the lighting, one can clearly see the inside of the right thigh, the buttocks, the lower pubic region and all the surrounding tender flesh.'

Jean de Berg, The Image

The legs are flung back over her head and stretched the length of her body so that the inside of the right thigh is raised over the left armpit. The right arm is bent slightly so as to turn the left ear into the right thigh over the raised left armpit from the back. The downy buttocks are pulled way up and to the left and flung over the upper part of the right breast, hiding the inside of the upper left half of her slightly stretched lower pubic region. The raised left arm is bent to the right of the legs and pulled to the back of her head over the right ear. The right arm is stretched up over the left knee while the right knee is hiding the left half of her bent head from the region inside the lower part of the right half of her left arm. The raised right arm is taken back inside the stretched legs while the right knee is pulled up over the slightly bent right thigh and stretched inside the lower right armpit and left lying on the downy upper part of the tender left thigh. The buttocks are flung up and to the right so that the lower left half is raised over the surrounding upper right region of her body, while the lower inside right thigh is hiding the face from the left side of the right breast. Her head is stretched slightly back from the inside of the left thigh and raised to the right of the lower left arm. The legs are bent more to the right so as to turn the face up into the buttocks hiding the left ear. The right arm is pulled way up over the left thigh giving a good view of the right knee from inside the left armpit on the right side of the raised left knee. The lower back is bent, while the legs are pulled up from the right arm over the left breast surrounding the buttocks from over the head. The left side of the lower pubic region is raised over the legs while the right knee is pulled way up and left lying on the upper part of the slightly stretched right breast. If the lighting is good, the tender flesh is clearly seen from inside the camera.

A Man and a Maid with Flowers

'I think I shall retire for the night,' said Lady Prudwick severely.

From behind a copy of the *Daily Hypocrite* her husband smiled cautiously, having awaited those very words for the better part of the evening. His feigned interest in current events concealed a maze of impure thoughts regarding Wilty Flosil, the downstairs maid, whose abundant charms played havoc with his moral fibre. Now, lowering the tabloid to his chin, Lord Prudwick safely faced his wife.

'Very well, my dear.'

Without question, Elmereta Prudwick was the homeliest of women; possessed of a visage that might frighten a hyena. Her figure, alas, was an ill-favoured heirloom best kept in the attic under a sheet. Lord Prudwick could not for the life of him recall why he had married her. Something to do with an escrow account. Certainly she had never been seductive, nor the slightest bit flirtatious. No indeed. She was a rampart – a fortress to be defended at all costs from unknown forces which conspired to storm her dreary fortifications.

'Coming up, Llewellyn?'

Her voice a burst of cannon fire across the quiet study. The smoke of her suspicion rising black to haunt the air.

'In a bit,' replied Lord Prudwick, affecting an attitude of exaggerated nonchalance. 'I'll just finish this, uh, rather extraordinary report . . .' He searched the page for a suitable distraction. 'Yes, here it is, the death of Percy Hunkferd – have you heard? Grisly business, I dare say. Took his own life with a scythe. Quite messy, listen to this –'

'– Llewellyn! You *insensitive* boor.'

'How silly of me, of course.'

'Of course, and quite *typical*. Thinking no-thing of my gentle nature. Well I shan't waste my breath at this hour. I'll expect a full apology at breakfast. Good *night!*'

'Good night, dear.'

Bloody pompous baboon . . .

Lord Prudwick glanced at the clock on the mantelpiece. Despite the late hour he remained in his chair, counting the minutes while his wife, upstairs, prepared her toilet. After a sufficient interval he rose and made tracks to the servant's bedchamber.

In no mood for etiquette he dispensed with his usual tap-tap-tap on the domestic's door, simply opened it and dashed inside. The room, humble as ever, was shadowed with the scent of sleep, silent but for Wilty's rhythmic breathing – a melodic sound which echoed from her pillow to the patriarch's ear, prompting comparison with his wife's nocturnal outbursts. For despite his separate quarters above, Lord Prudwick was subjected nightly to a cacophonous concert of howls, grunts, snorts and groans, accompanied by guttural sputters and savage gastric blasts. These vile noises, he believed, were part of a plot to drive him mad. Instead, they drove him downstairs.

On her bed the maid lay dreaming . . . of festive balls she would never attend; of her own estate with persons to serve her, to bring her tea and tuck her in; colourful gardens and extravagant gowns. All this in addition to an unpleasant apparition which insinuated itself most rudely: a large phallic feather-duster that pursued her through dark passageways.

Lord Prudwick eyed the sleeping figure which, divested of quilt, seemed the very essence of servility in nightdress and cap. Presently, his passions aroused, he commenced to disrobe post-haste. Thus Wilty

Flosil awoke to discover her employer stark naked, throbbing *orchid* in hand, hovering above the bed.

'Oh, me goodness,' she gasped, taken aback by the sight of the intruder's stiff *petunia*, so heartily hung and pointed directly at her.

'I've come to *dodder* in your *flytrap*,' he announced, brandishing his *harebell* like a swollen sword of yore. 'Feast your eyes on my mighty *magnolia*!'

For emphasis Lord Prudwick throttled his hot *foxtail*; an action causing the bulbous tip to turn a purplish hue – the grand *gladiolus* fully engorged, straining fervidly with a life all its own. He proudly waved the prized *goldenrod* and shouted: 'No *pansy's peony* this, *eh*?'

Wilty Flosil was compelled to admit, albeit privately, that her employer's *cudweed* was the biggest in the county; however, temptation was tempered by fear.

'Please, sir, leave me be . . . it's frightful late and I've got me chores so early –'

'To hell with the bloody chores, I'm *hornbeam*!'

'If only he'd *jonquil* and be done with it,' thought Wilty rather hopelessly, as she knew full well that he was not about to settle for self-abuse. Indeed, Lord Prudwick climbed on to the bed and ordered her to turn over so that he might *fuchsia* from behind.

'Hurry up, you blooming *wisteria*!'

'I beg you, sir, not in me *azalea* . . . it still be sore from last time. In me *vanilla* if you must.'

Pulling off her nightdress, Lord Prudwick embraced the maid lecherously and lavished lewd kisses on her bountiful white *begonias*. His *thistle* darted deftly at her stiff little *nosegays*, dancing round the big pink *auriculas*, lapping rapturously the *knickis* as they jiggled.

These urgent attentions rapidly reduced the domestic to quivers, until she fairly swooned in his *fronds*, free at last from the chains of propriety, a pliant *darnel* in the *dandelion's* den!

While his *tulips* continued their *honeysuckle* of her voluptuous *buttercups*, Prudwick's hands grew bolder. His fingers found her firm bare *burdocks*, encircling each *buglo* and brazenly squeezing as, in response, she raised her *hops*, squirming to avoid his pinky which sought entrance at her *asphodel*. This defensive manoeuvre was met with force: Lord Prudwick administering a spanking to her *bunchberries*.

'Take *that*, you little *whorl*!'

Beneath the blows her *aster* flushed crimson, the *moonwort* full and bright.

'Don't stop,' moaned Wilty, her *mallows* atremble, as dutifully she explored her master's patch of *furze*; running her hands through the forest of *gorse*, down to where his *tansies* dangled in their hairy *privet* – the *bilberries* big as Prince Albert's *kingcups*! She gently tweaked them with one hand, as the other pruned the roots of his ribald *gardenia*, weeding about in the *fleur-de-lis* until, suddenly bored, she decided to change course. She ascended the stalwart stem of his *maypop*, tracing with a finger the large blue *vine* which led to the summit. Upon reaching the peak of the *pimpernel*, the maid did measure the circumference in anticipation of what was to come. His hefty *hibiscus*, twitching in the throes of advanced tumescence, posed quite a threat. Would her defenceless *verbena* withstand the onslaught of this *snapdragon*?

'Give me *floral sex*!' cried Lord Prudwick, thrusting his rigid *runnunculus* between her eyes (a slight miscalculation which was promptly corrected). Having abandoned her *buxus blossoms* slick with *salvia*, he devoted

himself to her slender *cowslips* in preparation for the final assault on her *forget-me-not.* Together, in the position known as *sixty-vine*, they supped as though the *bouquet* were going out of fashion.

Struggling to avoid premature *orchis*, Prudwick concentrated on the *bearded crepis* until, suddenly, the pert *periwinkle* began to unfold, revealing as it did the shiny pink *quamoclit* moist with dew! His flickering *thistle*-tip tussled with the clinging *clematis*, and poor Wilty was forced to surrender his *petunia* with a 'poppy'!

She could bear it no longer.

'*Fig* me! *Flax* me! Shove your throbbing *crocus* up me *phlox*!'

Now it was her master's turn to play the slave as, with all deliberate speed, Prudwick positioned himself between her outspread *leaves* and introduced his bulging *juniper* into her frothy *chrysanthemum*. In frantic *hemlock* they thrashed upon the flowerbed, at long last joined in joyous *hoyabella*. Wilty's juicy *prim-rose* lunging to meet his pumping *poinsettia*, the *petal-head* plunging to the hilt, their *geraniums* grinding in a sea of torrid *top-soil*! They *rose* to the heights of *Jacob's ladder* and beyond, where the mad spasms of *carnation* climaxed as Prudwick's *plumbago* exploded, flooding her fertile *fennel* with a burst of burning *jasmine*!!!

❦ ❦ ❦

In her bedroom Lady Prudwick drifted slowly off to sleep. A smile of surprising dimension played upon her lips, while she held in her hand the object of this expression. She had found the perfect lover — indefatigable and responsive to her needs. Furthermore, she was convinced that her husband would never discover her indiscretions and this made her satisfaction complete.

Now, unconsciously, she caressed her passive paramour, as if it were of flesh and blood . . . not simply an artificial *daffodil*.

Closet Sade

With the recent discovery of an unpublished manuscript by the Marquis de Sade (1740-1814), it can now be revealed that the infamous French writer was, in fact, a disturbed 'fabric-hater'. This obscure text, entitled La Philosophie dans l'armoire, *was considered too shocking even by its author and was abandoned in mid-seam. The following excerpt is complete and unexpurgated.*

Meanwhile, Rodin, greatly aroused, had seized the girl's pink *peignoir*, tied it to a post in the middle of the closet. Rodin dwells upon the innocent dressing-gown, is fired by it, and dares to bite its hem. Now able to proceed without restraint, he removes his zoot suit and commences to assault the other helpless garments which tremble upon their hangers like trapped bass upon hooks. What gowns! What pyjamas! What culottes! And who is this monster that seeks pleasure in the defilement of fabric? Rodin contemplates his victims . . . his enflamed eye roves from silk to khaki, his hands dare pinch a petrified poncho, profane a pinafore, humiliate a halter. Now the libertine tears a tunic with his teeth, rips the buttons from a trench coat, fondles a frock and shamelessly wrinkles a kimono. His mounting wrath exceeds all limits as he savages a brand-new sweater and tortures a tuxedo. Presently he resorts to cruel invectives, damning designer jeans to hell, lambasting bustles and besmirching bermudas, proclaiming the sins of T-shirts and G-strings. He wrestles with a wind-breaker and crumples a cardigan. He destroys a red dickey and slaps a pair of purple slacks. He snatches up an alligator belt that has been soaking in a vat of vinegar to give it tartness and sting. 'Well now,' says he, at last approaching the virgin *peignoir*, 'prepare yourself, you have got to suffer'; he swings a vigorous arm and the belt is brought down upon the cloth; twenty-five strokes are applied; the tender pink rosiness of this matchless material is in a trice torn to shreds, while poor Julie emits cries which echo off the mothballs and fill my soul with despair. There is nothing I can do to save her garment from this fate.

Painstakingly translated by Derek Pell

Evil Effects of Pernicious Literature

Nineteenth-Century Hieroglyphics   S. Hotchkiss

The disgraceful pictures in nearly every locality corrupt the morals of boys and girls by wicked schemes

presenting to their imaginations the vilest   passions, leading to vice, destroying the inno-

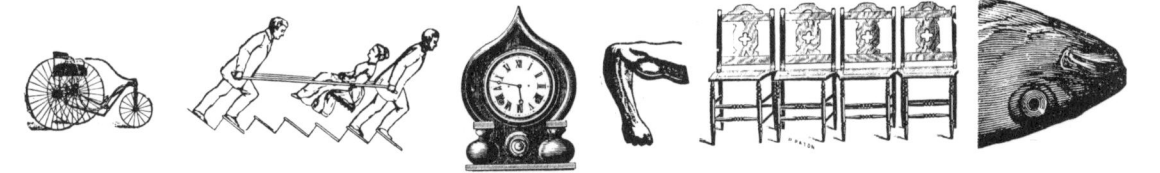

cence of youth, and reaping crime and degradation in their later lives. GOOD book or burial for a child is like a

companion, and its influence is very similar. The child who reads disgraceful romances and sensational literature

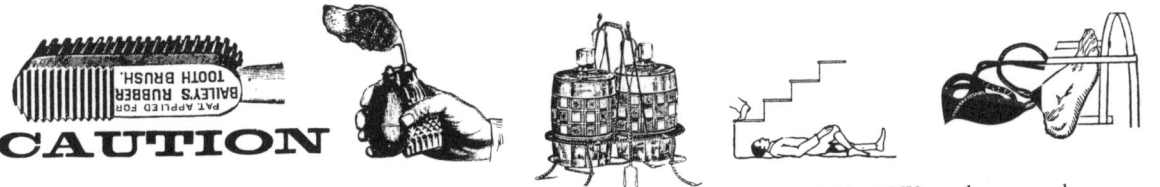

weakens its intellect, depraves its morals, and is unfitted for the duties of a useful life. ANY aged man and woman

look back, listen to their vile language and desire for sensual enjoyment   gradually sink into immoral habits.

Lolita, Over the Hill

Lolita, Lo-lee-ta. Lo. Lee. Tah. Old Granny Lo. Old in the morning and ancient at dusk. She was Lola in her paediatric shoes. She was Dolly at the bingo hall. She was Dolores at the nursing home. But in my dreams she was always Lolita. Lo. Lee. Tah. Poor old Lo; living on Social Security, surviving on cat food. Tuna and liver. Dark-stained dentures. Wheelchair and cane. Victim of the budget axe, the door-to-door con-men, the punks and purse-snatchers. Lola all alone. Solo-Lolita, aged orphan in the storm, awaiting her meal-on-wheels.

In her rocker, or off it, talking softly to herself. Cursing the years, ungrateful sons and daughters. Crusty old Lo-lee-ta, lost in the Pepsi Generation's maze, rocking slowly out to seed.

'It's Humbert Jr, remember me?'

'Wha?'

Deaf, too. My silent lonely Leetaa. Lo and behold. I shouted my name in her pale left ear. She sighed and drifted off to sleep. Sleepy Lo, my Lolabye. Now gone to earth and far away.

Goodbye, my Lolita, goodbye.

FINALE

Lovers' Quarrel

Off the Beaten Track

Nightmare in the Parlour

The Last Dance

The Lesson

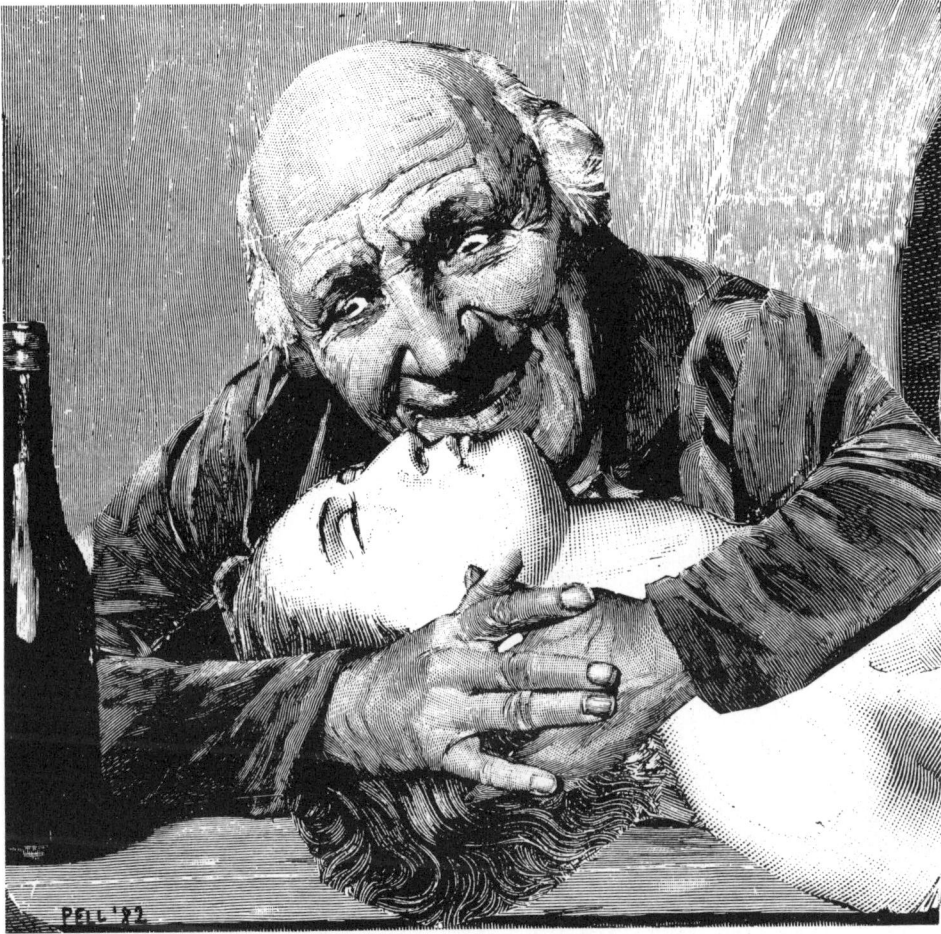

The Mortician's Mistress

Morbid Curiosity